Premonitions of the Past

SAMARTH SAWHNEY

INDIA • SINGAPORE • MALAYSIA

ISBN
Paperback 979-8-89744-615-5
Hardcase 979-8-89906-300-8

Contents

LOVE   33

ME?   65

Foreword

To hold a volume of poetry in one's hands is to hold a piece of the human soul, a delicate and intricate tapestry woven from emotions, thoughts, and experiences. And so it is with this collection of poems by Samarth, a young mind brimming with intellect and a heart overflowing with purity.

Samarth Sawhney's verses, crafted with a maturity beyond his years, reveal a profound understanding of the human psyche. They explore the depths of joy and sorrow, the complexities of love and loss, the wonder of the human intellect, and the enduring power of the human spirit.

I am proud to read his works and say that he is a product of his hard work and the values imbibed in him by his family and our school. Our school's efforts to bring out the best in our children is showcased through Samarth's intellect and creativity.

This collection is a testament to Samarth's keen observations, insightful reflections, and unique voice. His words resonate with an honesty and vulnerability that is both captivating and inspiring. Through these poems, we are invited to see the world through their eyes, to feel his emotions deeply, and to connect with the shared human experience on a profound level. His creations, Darkness and Me? showcase his profound depths of intellect and brilliant usage of vocabulary.

May these poems continue to inspire and uplift all who encounter them, a reminder of the enduring power of art to touch the soul and illuminate the human spirit.

From the Principal's desk,

Dr. Savita Arora

Principal

Bharti Public School, Delhi

Introduction

Hi, this is the author of this book. This book is written by me, a seventeen-year-old Indian boy, and it contains poetry about me facing and sometimes questioning my problems, which appear in my day-to-day life. I never imagined that one day you all would be reading the poetry I wrote for her and many others.

Have you ever thought of what death feels like or what happens after this soul departs the body? Is an evil person evil because of his past? What's the meaning of life? This book will make you think about things you may have never considered before. The book is divided into three parts, signifying three phases of life that I have gone through. Each poem is close to my heart, reflecting my motivations and emotions.

I have been inspired by the works of great poets like Robert Frost, John Keats, and Walt Whitman. I chose the title *Premonition of the Past* because it's an oxymoron and a wordplay. Premonitions are typically tied to the future, but by saying "premonition of the past," I am referring to memories—remembering the past and writing about it.

This book contains all the poems I wrote, both for others and for myself. I have tried to capture the raw essence of my feelings and thoughts in my work. This was my first time writing something like this, and I hope you enjoy reading it as much as I enjoyed writing it.

Once again, thank you so much for buying my book and showing support to an upcoming writer. I hope this book leaves an impact on you as much as it did to me.

For the Reader

Darkness

You know what is faster than the speed of light? Darkness because where light can't even reach darkness is present there. Darkness is the absence of light. It is also everywhere just for that light to go and it gets a chance to shine even in your life and with it we won't respect the real meaning of light. Darkness covers topics like *death, pain, life, hope and remorse.*

Love

Love, well, I love you love but what actually are you. Are you just a feeling we feel when we are attracted to one or is it just a chemical reaction in our brain so that we don't forget to create offspring. For me love is her. She was my love, my moon. This part of my life is filled with some of my happiest and some of my saddest poems I wrote for her that contain attraction, love and heartbreak.

Me?

This is the last part of my book and is about myself. It's the last because if you both mix the prior parts darkness and love you will get me. It is about my suffering, how I was surrounded with friends, love and light and in the end how it was all taken away from me. It's a reflection of my true self in the form of poems. You have to read this part to understand the complex feelings of broken relationships, backstabbing, and why do I write?

     FOR THE READER

DARKNESS

Broken Mirror

"I have been broken into several pieces.

Dreamed of so many scared faces,

Asking me, 'Am I alright?'

For me all might seem to have similar looks.

Why feels they have seen my every nook.

One day, might create some popular books.

Until then, will write poems with stupid hooks.

but sometimes a light crosses my mind,

Who were the people looking at *me*?"

What's the Meaning of Life

Life, Is it to find a loving wife?

Or is there no reason to thrive?

The idea might make you strife.

Each day open my searching eyes,

Read works of philosophers not alive.

Some say it's God, or a divine Paradise[1],

Is death the real truth, then give me a knife.

I've gone through so many sleepless nights

Just to know, am I even right to write?

But not alone in these searching times,

Even the wisest men were surprised,

Because even they didn't know the meaning of life...

---

1 A place of eternal peace in christianity.

Dead Subway

Just imagine you meet your fatal end.

Now you open your eyes in an empty train.

No one in that coach; might be your transcend.

Your life has changed. Do you still have a brain?

The metro stops at an unknown station.

You get off, searching for your own race,

Just to find no one in this inhabited place.

You are the king of this lonely nation.

You are there, with only one bench to sit, in *end*,

Thinking what happened: is this hell or heaven?

Why don't I have a scar, which I got when eleven?

Stuck there, waiting for another tube to come for your

descent.

Ship of Theseus[2]

We travel so far, still it never stumbles.

Journey after journey, we changed its parts.

From the mighty storm to the bumpy sea,

It carried us on its back, safe from the lurking danger.

First came the bow, then the keel, and lastly the hull—

all drifted apart.

We advanced so long, yet it didn't trip.

Voyage after voyage, we transformed its bits.

From the ferocious typhoon to the rough ocean,

It bore us up, docked, protected by hidden risks.

Initially came the head, then the bottom, finished by

the skeleton; each bobbed away.

---

2 Ship of Theseus is a thought experiment originated from ancient Greece , that asks whether an object is the same if all of its original parts are replaced over time.

Corruption

They say, why shouldn't we run from our duty?

Hard-earned money shoved down the drain so deep,

Or worse, in unworthy pockets it sleeps.

For the fake pledge they took, screams

Of lies and deceit and useless schemes.

So true. But still, if you roll back the time

To see, taxes were not just a futile fine.

It was a means to ensure a strong line

Of bones that bring stability to our spine.

Pain

Pain—some people laugh to make it half.
Many, to ease it, look at past photographs.
Others try to hide it from their kind,
but in pain, your mind becomes blind.

Pain, a staple in my life, everywhere I go.
Now, it's my only friend that won't flow.
Even if I cry, it won't sink low,
So let's just live with this eternal sorrow.

Face Is the Index

Some say, "Face is the index of mind."
Who says that might be wrong because,
To find real feelings, to know if they are kind,
Why to judge from the mask God designed?

You may ask, "Would you like the presence of a man
With a large scar and larger hands,
In a pub where everyone is a Red flag?"

You know It surely can be deceptive,
Because I've seen many murderers wide smiles,
And persons with a messed-up face is just their style.

Fallen Angel

Might just be a star, stranded from his glory.

Just wait to let him die down, or stand to listen to his story.

Even the god of hell fell from the heaven,

Then who am I to cry like I am seven?

There is a saying that when life gives you lemons...

The last part, I might have forgotten.

But this fallen angel will not get rotten.

Feudal Lord[3]

My beautiful Feudal lord, he is so pretty, we treat him as our saviour.

My poor Feudal lord eats well every night but can't afford for us.

My religious Feudal lord, it's okay for him to go to church, but he is our only god.

My lazy Feudal lord sleeps soundly when we suffer and work in his field.

My unforgiving Feudal lord punches our wives when she tries to stop his assault.

My savage Feudal lord makes us strip down in the cold winter to prove our loyalty.

---

3 Person who controlled territory in 9th century europe.

My cruel Feudal lord doesn't think once before sending
peasants to be beheaded in war.

My Feudal lord doesn't feel the pain which his
branding[4] has caused.

My dead Feudal lord looks so quiet without his head,
peacefully lying on the ground.

---

4 A method to mark slaves.

Death's Diary

On a rainy day of winter that made my thoughts
hinder.

It's been a long weekend of work; got all the people off
the list.

But still, feel empty and crave a sense of bliss.

Fucked up, I know, by taking this job. It's hard to be
death;

A snap of your finger can stop any heartthrob.

I die from inside every time I slit a throat,

Started to write the names in my diary to take notes.

Can't stop thinking about the child taken from her
mother.

Wish they can meet in a separate life with each other.

Waiting for the Dawn

Me, sitting still, thinking of ways to kill

That person in front of the mirror, who loves to hunt.

His own happiness, by sabotaging his life, just to
camouflage[5] and rife,

By shaving the people that care and inviting fake
friends who can't dare to hear.

He tries to lead to his own demise, but is afraid to say
his final goodbyes,

To the loved ones, full of agony because of his low
sanity and guarantee,

That in his next dawn, he will not be a minor pawn[6],

And will take the hardest path, no matter how many
thorns.

---

5 Disguise.

6 Is a chess piece of lowest value.

Losing Hope

"Losing my hope like a drop from a cliff.

Will they save me, pump blood in something stiff?

Can't get a hold, sinking in a bottomless pit.

Why do I try every crevice, beating my body to fit?

Hard to breathe here, eyes closing, may call it quits."

Why So?

"God created a silly human, why so?

If he could only do right, why so?

Just for him to waste it all, why so?

A life full of pain and agony, why so?

He is addicted to validation why so?

Gave power to question him, why so?"

Ash

Why does everything return to ash?

Even the sun's fire douses in the ocean.

Light as a feather still holds many souls,

Might burn one day, turn into dark dust.

Brittle; don't touch, or it might break.

Grey, different from heavenly beauty.

Consume and get to know who I am,

Or think, debate on words but don't undermine.

Kill yourself; let phoenix[7] bring new life.

---

7 A flaming bird related to rebirth.

Past Remorse

Life is so beautiful and dark at times.

Just can't imagine what will be next.

We can just look behind and regret:

Why am even living in this life ?

Pathetic paths pave us, so live it once.

Past people go away—I just want to talk

What happened to what we called friendship?

O brother of mine Did it die, or maybe not?

Alone in This World

Why always alone, searching for love?

Feels incomplete as a flightless dove[8].

Do I need a protector for my abused heart?

Find myself in a mirror, broken apart.

---

8 Pigeon

God Complex

I am your saviour, so worship me as your god.

Teaching you, perching—understand, not a fraud.

No hell or heaven, just infinity, so

That's why you might find me odd.

Pray to me as if I were your lord,

A knight in armour with a shining sword.

My psychologist made me assured;

created it all, so give me an applause.

Regional? Just a myth—open your eyes, give me awards.

Legacy—I began it all. Don't believe it? Check my records.

Me and all my twelve friends are outlawed,

for having something called last supper[9] with my squad.

---

9 It's the last meeting of Jesus with his disciple.

LOVE

Spots

I drowned in her hazel eyes,
Ruby lips, reason for my demise.
Hair fragrant, made me fainted,
Her smile seems to be painted.
Can't see, doused in her dreams,
Skin so bright, it shines and gleams.

When the sun shines on my moon,
Even corpses could look from their tomb[10].

But the moon isn't perfect without her spots.

---

10 A structure for remains of dead bodies

Just a Beautiful Face

The most beautiful girl I have ever seen,

Her face was made up of perfection.

By just seeing her beauty, my heart fades away;

hope she gets everything she asks for.

Her name, given by her parents, suits her flawlessly.

Like a fairy, she came into my life; I wish she never

leaves me.

At this magical time, she is the only thing that brings

me a smile.

First Steps

In a blooming flower, the smell of love

Can't be compared to anything in the world.

Like dew drops on a blade of grass,

It's the time that slips at last. When

You are with them, your heart pounds,

By a slick of touch, your feelings drown.

In shadows and light, through seasons we grow,

A journey together, where only we know.

In every scar etched, there's a story to tell,

Of a love that is timeless, of a truth that compels.

Through trials and triumphs, we walk hand in hand,

Creating a story that's perfectly planned.

Or so we think but nobody knows what's the legacy

Maybe it won't be that bad so let us make a step to our

destiny.

Foggy Road

Once again, I stood in front of a foggy road,

Wanting you to hold my hand, to make it glow.

So we can start a journey for as long as time;

I will support and always protect you from behind.

Love can't be understood—it's a flame that can't be
blown.

Her pearly smile became my lifeline because,

When I see her, my heart sings a hundred rhymes.

They say you shouldn't rush in with your feelings,

But darling, I can't help myself—I'm falling in love.

First Love

One of the oldest feelings felt:

To paint her image on my heart,

Just for it to be torn apart.

So foolish, thinking she might stay.

They say first love can't fade away.

Can't chip it down; the heart will bleed.

This age won't see what I sought.

Don't love the form; her soul must be pure.

I Loved Once

" It's a long story,

Which couldn't be expressed.

I also loved once

Daydreaming about her

Was my favourite hobby,

I also loved once

So perfect, was afraid

To tell my feelings.

Lost her even before,

Could do something,

I also loved once

Way out of my league.

But as they say,

My love was blind.

So I also loved once"

Her Eyes

Her eyes—could write thousands of lines.

Those eyes felt warm; was it because

I was comfortable with them watching?

Her eyes had a blue tint,

Which seemed to drown me.

We used to talk with our eyes,

But now, those eyes will never see me again.

Not because she left, but because

Those eyes are positioned with love.

If I look into them, once again fall I will

But this time, you won't. So Better not to look.

Confession from the Past

Is it a new start?
Wake up, and my mind is in parts.
Am in love but can't open up my heart.

There are reason that's holding me back:
Don't know what to do, is there any hack?
Just want to feel love, which my past lacks.

Told myself several times to not fall,
But don't even know why I smile when you call.
can listen to your voice until dawn.

Want you, but this is not the right time.
My feelings are confused like these rhymes.

True Love

You know where we find pure love?

In the hearts where you can't think about

Someone else, even for the blink of an eye.

From the lids closing to the sun shining,

You wait for those few minutes in a day

Where she could smile for you and only you.

Her pain is mine, till I write it on paper full of spite.

Like wet clay, you mould yourself in her image.

She is stuck in mind at an inescapable maze.

Eternal Bliss?

Love is a feeling nobody understands,

An emotion even the hermit[11] can't comprehend.

A reaction in our brain, by founding the motherland,

Or is it an eternal bliss that I misunderstand?

It's a contraband[12] which my body reprimands.

---

11 Sage with lots of knowledge.

12 A banned item.

Toxic Chain

Why did you come into my life?

Just to show me your darkest side.

Thought you could fix me; you were the same.

Want to ask, why did you hug me so tightly that day,

With those hateful hands I held?

Those hands, they were poisoned.

Poisoned with the pain I felt,

Had to break that toxic chain.

You killed the happiness inside my brain.

Called off this fucked bond,

Not to make you suffer,

But my agony needed to end.

Want answers: do you hate me?

Well, that's clearly to see, because

I see your new name, 'Instagram user[13].'

---

13 Name after getting blocked by someone.

Alone

Stand alone, looking for a path in the mist,

My aching hand is sore from holding her tight.

In the end, it was all for plight and sorrow;

Can't handle this solemn anymore for years.

Seek that fine tune so can dance in peace,

But nothing falls on my deaf and dear ear.

Wrong Man

She loved the wrong man,

Couldn't be as pure as she can.

Not a mistake of that beauty,

That man is always a whore,

Staking others for attention,

While she blocks them all.

Then why does he cry at night,

When he only pulled the call?

Cursed Love

Why am I cursed with no one in my life?
Don't know why it hurts to pull that knife.
Deep down, my heart cries a mournful song;
The journey is full of problems—right or wrong.

Can't remember when I last smiled for a soul.
Leaving them all behind—no fucking goal.
Drowning in alcohol to sober my sombre pain,
Yet every sip just deepens the red stains.

Forever Friendship

That girl I used to see every day was a good friend,

But destiny made it so, as if to break us, to change everything.

Was so sad and heartbroken but didn't have the guts to confess to her

That she was the secret I was hiding.

After that, our paths crossed again,

But everything had changed—we were strangers.

For me, had to distance myself from her to let the feelings die.

And they did. It doesn't mean that we can't be friends again.

I'm happy to find a friend can talk to when I feel low.

She understands me, and I try to understand her.

We were meant to be friends.

Rejection

You are not the one I was searching for.
Was stupid, falling for your flaws.
My only mistake was didn't foresee that
You never loved me like I used to do.

Was I just a toy for you to screw?
That was the final straw when you mocked me so free.
You can't let go, it's clear to see—
Is that why all your talk revolves around me?

In the end, I'd love to say, you lost the chance
With me to share a romantic dance.
Notice how you keep stealing a quick glance—
Hence, for your quiet notice, you can't advance.

Waiting for a Move

Keep on watching the ticking clock,

There's a fear that I have been blocked.

Spent my time thinking your heart is hard as rocks,

I'm not the person who will stalk, but I just want you to

stop.

"Fuck it," you said to me while breaking everything up.

That day, I saw your new face, which was filled with

hatred.

In your deck of cards, there is no trump,

Because I am far from your intoxication.

She left me at that point when I needed her most,

Wanted to show her that now she is just a ghost.

Why couldn't do anything without being opposed?

Saw Her Today

Such a nice face but has the darkest past.

Immediately got uncomfortable with her presence at
last

In my life She came in a quiet terrible phase

She has only one toxic trait, by playing the victim she
can persuade.

Was sure like a lizard she would change her feelings.

Every time I look at her, my past gives me a verbal
beating.

Ask, "How can you look me in the eyes?" While an
unpleasant meeting.

What you have done to me was more than any kind of
cheating.

That day I promised myself to never commit

Not ever try to explain my feelings like a ferocious
vomit.

Would not ever be able to trust again never to leave my
orbit[14]

You were just like other people who murdered me with
fake comments.

---

14 Fixed trajectory.

One Lost Girl

Saw a lost girl, lost in her world,

Beauty can't explain her face.

How could God create herself,

But better eyes filled with tears?

Didn't know I hugged for the last;

Still got scratches on my back.

Kissed that Bella, so my soul left,

Happy that it was ended, for

I didn't deserve to hold her hand.

My Moon

I called her my crescent moon,

Didn't know she would disappear too.

Her beauty unmatched, voice a croon[15];

Fumbled his queen—such a big loon[16].

Even the gods couldn't make a tune

That could match her face, lost too soon.

Some may call her a boon, my love in attune;

She was my monsoon in the month of June.

---

15 humming.
16 Stupid.

Recent Heartbreak

You left, still I won't ever hurt you with my words.

It hurts to close them, swollen from the salt.

But truth be told, in darkness, I see her smiling.

Can't fathom the last time we hugged was the last time.

Why do I see you in my dreams, happy with me?

Didn't Want You to Go

Didn't want you to go, but life...

He will be happy, but not anymore.

It's okay, as they say, true love doesn't just die.

So I won't.

It will be hard to live without any texts from someone

dear to my heart,

But it's okay; to experience this was a gift.

To be loved like never before was something

Thought I would never experience it.

Will Not Stop Loving

Why can't I move on from you?
Didn't we both hold each other?
But you are gone, that's not a lie.

But why is it hard for me to forget
The time we spent? I only wish to
See you happy, with or without me.

Do you also feel the pain? Even after
I cry, my heart doesn't want to deny
That you won't come back into my arms.

But as a last hope,
I still wear it on my hands,
As a shackle or a band.

Seasonal Love

In the icy, cold season of winter,

My phone rang to notify me about a star,

Different from others, connected through

A bond that went forever, but only lasted a few
seconds.

With irony, I lost the way to zenith[17];

Now, how could I see my star?

It rained yellow in the season of autumn,

Just like her, to fall into my arms,

In a way I had never even thought before.

But as a menace to my own happiness,

Broke that lovely, but withered rose into pieces,

Burned into dust, blown away to an endless abyss[18].

---

17 Highest point.
18 Void.

In the damned season of monsoon,

She came into my life, barging all the doors.

Fell for her, but she never even wobbled.

Like a shuttle, she launched me into space,

Told me I was a guy she could marry.

My Last Kiss

My last kiss was so amazing.

We both looked at each other in amazement.

She accepted me for what I was.

We were listening to our favourite songs.

It was so unexpected that I couldn't have imagined it.

It's the cure for my improving illness,

Made me so happy, even if I miss her now.

It filled my life with the warmth I crave.

Took the early steps and never could look back.

It tasted of cherry, strawberry, and her.

Dreams of Past

See, in my dreams, only you can be found.

Is that the reason why you are so profound?

See myself holding your hand till dawn,

In the background, Cupid[19] plays his love horns.

Why can't my dream be real, I ask myself.

Are the feelings true; can you only heal me.

You are the only person seen in my eyes,

That's the reason, maybe—only want you. Would
never let you cry.

The cutest girl I know—I act childish around your
presence,

Because I don't feel vulnerable or judged by your
essence.

Really feel sad because of your absence;

You are like a sweet present to end this sentence.

---

19 God of love.

I just want us to relive the moments we passed together,

And there's something pending between us too—I hope you remember.

Don't Leave Me

Don't leave me for doing something damned.

It is not easy to make connections for me.

Won't search for others just to replace you.

Why would someone give so much love, you ask?

They say, will destroy myself behind the trail.

So be it. Let me pour alcohol into my system,

Utile it stop from my rust and maybe fail,

Write the stuff wanted to be inked on me.

Because I love, so please let me go into

Your dreams, where we can meet.

ME?

Dark Night

Was standing in the darkest night.

They believe it's because of a fight.

Don't know if I was wrong or right.

Why do I care despite her not being polite?

But I've made mistakes, that's my plight.

Now I seek to mend, to become bright.

In the depths, I'll ignite my own light.

Black Crocs

Still remember that day I lost it.

It was passed down by my family—

Those loosely fitted black crocs.

A sunny day so hot it could melt dreams,

At the railway station, crowded as ever.

People looked giantess to my small eyes.

Lost those crocs; I cried that day,

Not because of those departed crocs,

But because my identity became that of a stray dog.

They might get a new owner who loves them more.

How would I bear the loss of my loosely fitted crocs?

Still want to go to the same station,

To see if those crocs fit me.

But it's too late, because I have lost them now.

     PREMONITIONS OF THE PAST

I Saw Myself

Today, I saw myself in a mirror.

He was standing in front,

Like a reflection but real.

Same voice, with the same tone.

I tried to talk, but I was stopped.

From his end, I just was a stranger.

I know that boy wouldn't have talked, because he was
the old past I hate.

But still, looking at him made me happy,

To know how much I have gained.

How much people around me have changed,

Supported by his peers. Wish I was too.

Oh Brother

My brother, why do you fight?

Thought I had something great with you,

But good things don't last.

Will he come back and say sorry?

If not, it's okay; I'm happy with our memories.

A girl came into our life and separated us.

Was it my mistake, or you were in the dirt?

Why Do I Write

"Why am I writing these stupid lines?
Doesn't even make sense to me now.
Is it my shattered, bleeding, broken heart?
Or to ease my pain, because she left me?
Like, to get attention or to rhyme things?

Just getting the idea from my stupid head,
Mostly about death, darkness and pain.
You want me to make happy rhymes.
But how to preach something I've never experienced."

The Monster

They call me a monster; the assumption is correct.

Yes, I am a devil ; just can't hide my face.

Now will fight for myself and others with grace,

Never let anybody backstab, or to never be replaced.

You can see me in yourself, learning your every move,

Replicating them as if I were you—that's the whole
truth.

You can run for eternity; I will never be removed.

My life will be changed when I find my second half.

Then I will be at peace; my anger will change to a loud
laugh.

I was so angry that even my god is scared of me;

He just wants me to leave him so he can be free.

Everything Will Be Alright

Used to have a phrase when I was a child,
Which was used more than my smile:
In the end, everything will be alright.

But it never, ever manifested in my life.
When I sniff some music, it gives me a nice high.
One day, might overdose on things that makes this boat
float.

Life is a street fight in which you always die.
No matter how hard you struggle, your existence will
be erased.
There is no hope; this coin toss is one-sided.
It's okay to die peacefully rather than suffer what this
world gives.

Which gives me a new perspective on this sentence:

That everything will be alright in the end.

 PREMONITIONS OF THE PAST

Return of the Prodigal Son

The time was when all the stars were in line.

Returned to let his people know that he was
intertwined,

By mistake and sorrow, he couldn't save his friend's
life.

Saddened by this calamity, he cried that day from his
real eyes.

Deemed as the prodigal[20] son who went to sort
everything out,

Didn't come home because he was so distraught by the
loud shout.

In his head, the only way he could find peace and love
was the holy ground.

Got to know about a voyage every being tries to find.

---

20 A person who left his home. (Mostly young boys)

Some call it enlightenment, some say it's just a myth.

The path he took was hard and full of hurdles.

It was a shame that he couldn't; the result was like a
fruit with just its pit.

The return was as disappointing as drinking milk that
has curdled.

Perfect Man

Trying to be the perfect man will kill me one day.

Trying to save every falling peer will surely lead to my demise.

Trying to be absolute at everything will start my downfall.

Trying to fake a smile at every occasion in my life will kill me one day.

Trying to impress the masses timelessly will kill me one day.

Trying to be an impostor to fit into every shape will kill me one day.

Trying to lift the imaginary weights of supporting my family will kill me one day.

Trying to maintain a physique that doesn't allow me to eat will kill me one day.

Trying to suppress my emotional baggage will kill me
one day.

The addiction to seek perfection will kill me one day.

Dark Slumber

Everybody in life leaves me in a dark slumber.

People mostly go away in the month of September.

But people don't define me; my god does.

Oh shit, my saviour died a long time ago.

Am building a garden for myself of chocolate, peaches,
and roses

And flushing my past, which is haunted with unwanted
memories, closet.

A park they won't get to enjoy,

Leaving me will surely get them destroyed.

Or am I the one cutting the string of voice?

Many people came, stayed, and left by their own
choice.

Reflection

"I can't see my reflection in the mirror. Why so?

Maybe stopped looking for it.

Or successfully converted into another man.

Perhaps shed my skin because of them.

But certainly, this is not the past.

Still, where has it gone, stolen?

Did I kill it with my own two hands?"

Son to Father

Father, that couldn't be mine? Why?

O great man, imposing false hope.

Can't understand, both are not alike.

We might share blood, but not the soul.

Don't want to return to a house that once was called home.

There's a gap between us that will never be filled.

Might be the age, or might just be the hill.

Sleepless Night

"I have started to have some sleepless nights.
In the darkness, search for a beam of light.
When I lay down, my brain starts to fight.

My brain peaks to imaginary heights.
Visualise myself fighting as an iron knight.
Contemplate what is wrong and right.

It's likely I am the only person,
And the whole world is quiet.
Or it's the deafening silence before a riot.

I have started to have..."

Real Friends

Why couldn't I make real friends?

They Might go away to others.

Or do I drive them insane?

Hurt bad, can cry a crystal river

But unlikely don't have a shoulder.

Bitter taste of a victorious loss left me stranded.

But still at what cost?

What did I do to deserve this fate?

Lose them as flies, blink and go.

Stranger again will ask a question

Why don't people like broken men?"

SAMARTH SAWHNEY

Life

As the sun sets, you look in my direction.

Eyes closed, arms open, seeking perfection.

Just thinking of my time upon this globe

Filled your life with a glimpse of hopeless hope.

Maybe not truth to be kept in a box;

Open it by your choice, or it is to be lost

For eternity, in the void called life.

Am I a Bad Guy

"Am I a bad guy for letting their tears flow?

Am I a bad guy for breaking my solemn vow?

Am I a bad guy for killing the beautiful crows?

Am I a bad guy for targeting black snow?

Am I a bad guy for misunderstanding her tone?

Am I a bad guy for picking up the wrong bone?

Am I a bad guy for ignoring her when in need?

Am I a bad guy for spreading stories of awful deeds?

Am I a bad guy in the process of retaining sins?

Am I a bad guy so let me be or talk to me it's your choice?"

SAMARTH SAWHNEY

Grey

Just can't hold it anymore now.

Can't live a life I don't like.

Might just take my own,

Or will they have the honour?

My blood, when it's touched air,

Turned black like the outer world,

Where they cry in front but laugh at back.

Not so pure to have fake friendship.

Happy to live alone without any strings.

It's Lonely at the Top

They say it's lonely at the top,

And I haven't even started.

But still, I can count them all

On my sliced hand, bloody red,

By all who left to pursue their bonds.

Why do we seek them, who left us hanging?

Maybe they also knew that they couldn't be carried

For the journey from fire and ice that paves the way

To my success, but I ask myself:

Is being second better than having a severed hand?

And if the latter is right, why should we fight?

Because, as they say, no soul would survive, only the
one could thrive.

Takes blood and sweat to sit on the throne of thorns
that's why it's the place no one won't.

Death

Can't even feel myself now;

My skin may have turned blue.

Toes and fingers numb with broken bonds,

just a carcass left behind.

My own skin won't fit me now

On this dreadful globe.

To rot every day and suffer,

Everything just dammed.

With the water way above,

Like a fallen angel and his might,

I have started to lose my gleaming smile.

Walking towards a brewing storm,

Not knowing when to stop and treat my wounds.

I Am Still Standing

I am still standing, no matter what.

Won't give them happiness.

My eyes flame with pure red rage.

Can't explain life, so why waste it

By crying over things that won't stay?

Think I suffer from stumbling on my legs?

Even my smile can eat them whole.

Bumps came, and fell into a dark ditch,

But remember that I am still standing.

Did I?

I did everything, but still no light.

But still, I won't lose my shining smile.

They think they can reckon someone,

Still, they don't know a broken mirror.

A punch would only land with pain.

Promised one that I can't lose myself,

So I will not—for her and for her smile.

Train of Joy

We got to a train full of joys.

Want to listen to that sweet "Ahoy!"

Of birds chirping to a happy place.

A white blanket surrounds our stupid Grace.

My solace, some say, is a generous escape.

So, let it be in my heart, thousand miles apart.

But still, when I see my happy play,

My life turns into a shining Grace.

Afterlife

When I open my eyes,
a mystery bird closes the gates behind.
In a sandpit, I tumble to find

nothing but a heart beating alive,
to get what they seek in their life,
all to be compared to the light.

And if it's the right time,
they might witness the afterlife.

Diary of a Broken Man

Nobody likes a broken man,
Severed string from above.
Hell or heaven can't rule him.

Surrounded by a blue blanket,
Can't pull it, or he'll get cold feet.
As closer he gets, the line blurs.

Maybe this time, he won't regret
Cutting his wound again, so they
Can see that he also bleeds the same.

Writers Dilemma

How does the artist die?

Laughed at for his words,

Or even shot in the head?

When his work isn't seen,

By busy thinking beings,

While it was alive, nobody tried.

Many were put in the oven,

Or even some burned alive—

Many left off the streets to die,

And others so famous, killed by a drive-by.

Facing "justice" to drink what they sought,

Some go insane, while others destroy their thoughts.

This is the writer's dilemma: that maybe

His ideas would find the light,

And that's the day of shine when the writer dies.

Conclusion

What started as a side project became so prominent in my life that I couldn't leave it for even a second (even when my teachers scolded me for studying, but you know!). I always felt compelled to work on it, no matter what. Even during the hardest of times, I found myself writing as a way to release my stress. This journey has truly changed my perspective on life.

My main motive was to create poems that would make the reader reflect on profound topics—life, death, love, friendship—the things we either overlook or take for granted. If, even for a fraction of a second, this book made you think about the subjects mentioned within, then I have achieved my goal.

I wanted to spread awareness about the darker aspects of life that cannot be ignored. Life is not simply divided into black and white; it is a spectrum of grey, and that is what I've tried to convey through my work.

Acknowledgment

Firstly, thank you for reading my book. I truly hope you enjoyed it as much as I did creating it.

This book would not have been possible without the efforts of my mother and sister, who dedicated their soul and time to my upbringing. They truly were my backbone and supported me at every stage of my life. I cannot express how happy I am to be able to give back even a fraction of what you both have done for me. Love you both so much.

I also extend my heartfelt thanks to Mr. Sarthak Paliwal for empowering me and encouraging me to break some of my boundaries. It was your effort that brought my book to the shelf.

Last but not least, I am deeply grateful to my friends. You all know who you are! Without your support, I could never have imagined myself writing this book. Thanks a lot!